# The Art of Being Preserved

Eleni Sophia

The Art of Being Preserved– Eleni Sophia

Copyright © 2025 Eleni Sophia

The Art of Being Preserved

All rights reserved.

ISBN: 978-1-914275-59-3

Perspective Press Global Ltd

The Art of Being Preserved— Eleni Sophia

## DEDICATION

Thank you, God, for always blessing me and for making me such a lucky girl <3

Devotions for the God-led woman. A book you can open anywhere, trusting that every page will speak to your soul.

The Art of Being Preserved– Eleni Sophia

كن السهولة في صعوبة أحدهم
*Be the ease in someone's hardship*
**– God is Her Bestie**

The Art of Being Preserved— Eleni Sophia

**Worthiness** - remembering who you are
**Returning Home** - healing in solitude
**Becoming *Her*** - the woman God called you to be
**The Art of Being Preserved** - sacred timing and union

## Worthiness

You must be a woman who knows her worth, because when you walk in your value, nothing can phase you. When you walk knowing who you are, you carry a strength many quietly wish they had but cannot embody - and in possessing this, you'll often encounter those who project their fears onto you. But when you understand yourself, you align with who God created you to be, and in doing so you gain the awareness to rise above it all. You walk through life knowing their limiting beliefs are not yours, knowing you were created for something bigger. He made you an anomaly, set apart to share your magic in this world. The sacredness you possess gives you the ability to be in direct communication with your Creator, and your intuition becomes sharper than ever.

She trusts that what is meant for her will always find her, and that God will guide her toward everything written in her name. This is for the woman in her self-discovery era, where her softness is her quiet strength and her devotion her greatest power.

## The Art of Being Preserved– Eleni Sophia

**Become your own muse.**

To attract a love that is completely in awe of you, you must be in awe of yourself. To attract a life you are mesmerized by you must be mesmerized by your daily actions. In becoming your own muse, you understand that you are your best passion project, and every day becomes an opportunity to refine the masterpiece that you are.

When you're a woman who knows her life's timing isn't ruled by the noise around her, when your faith is the root of your power and you walk with complete certainty that it's all working out for you, I hope you know you've been chosen by God. The courage it takes to say 'no' when the entire world conforms, but you know you're here for something greater, is powerful.

When the world's chaos no longer shakes your peace, you rise into a higher level of womanhood. You become the woman who changes generations after her; a sanctuary is found within you. You create a life where solitude feels like peace, where your mind is at ease, and where wellness becomes worship. You move with clarity in who you are. You fear nothing because you are guided. You know that every voice that calls your dreams unrealistic is simply trying to trap you in their cage, and the world's approval becomes unnecessary.

The Art of Being Preserved– Eleni Sophia

So, every day, become a woman you are completely, entirely, and exclusively in awe of. In doing so, you become your own muse.

### The Art of Being Preserved— Eleni Sophia

Please take the time to understand yourself, because if you don't, the world will try to tell you who you are. You were never created to fit into their version of you; you were created to walk in God's. There is an innate power in choosing yourself every day, not the version expected of you, because your life was never meant to be understood by everybody. The more you lean into who your Creator made you to be, the freer you become. You stop living for approval and start living in alignment. You stop apologizing for your light and start walking in it fully.

## The Art of Being Preserved— Eleni Sophia

You're such a sweet girl, and I think you've been in an environment that pulled you away from your authentic self so much that you forgot how precious you truly are. The way you've been treated is not a reflection of your worth, and it never will be. Your only task now is to stay soft. To keep your heart open. To trust that no matter who leaves, you can still send love their way. To know that even when the lesson was painful, you don't have to speak bitterly about the person who was once your everything. This chapter was never meant to break you; it was meant to awaken you. It was simply part of your journey, a sacred reminder to never settle again, to listen to your intuition, and to return to the woman you are when the world is quiet. One day, you will be held in the tenderness of someone who sees you exactly as you are: steady, gentle, rare. But until that day comes, your work is to live in harmony with who your Creator is calling you to be, not with the expectations of others or the roles you took on to feel loved. Take each day slowly, with grace, and let it bring you closer to remembering your truth. You may have lost sight of her for a while, but that girl within you is still there. She's patiently waiting for you to notice her again. It's okay to come back home to yourself. It's okay to release the parts that became heavy, to soften where you had to be strong, to trust your own rhythm again. And as you do, listen for that quiet voice inside you, the one that never left, the one that has always known her way back.

## The Art of Being Preserved– Eleni Sophia

The woman who lives her life intentionally doesn't allow the noise of the outside world to pour into her home. And when I say home, I mean the peace she's created in her mind and heart. If you want to cultivate a life of fulfilment, listen to the voice within. No one ever looks back wishing they had listened to others. They only wish they had listened to themselves. Never let anyone make you feel bad for the choices you make for yourself: for the boundaries you set, for the peace you protect, and for the life you are co-creating with your Lord. When you're the black sheep, do you really expect others to understand you? When you've taken the time to know yourself, to understand your own heart, to walk closely with God, the entire world could stand against you and you would still feel safe, because you know you're covered by the most powerful source.

## The Art of Being Preserved– Eleni Sophia

Every time you resist temptation, heaven takes note. One thing about God, He never lies. The Quran says, 'Good women are for good men, and good men are for good women.' The Bible says, 'A good man brings good things out of the good stored up in his heart.' So, what now? Your external world will always mirror your inner world. When you choose to create peace within your mind, your life becomes a reflection of this peace. You are rare. With intentions as pure as yours, of course God is going to give you the best. He's just testing to see if you'll cave. You were never meant to belong to everyone. You were destined for one man; the one God is preparing for you. So, when you start questioning your worth, come back to this and remember the power you carry in simply being yourself.

## The Art of Being Preserved– Eleni Sophia

God doesn't hide to punish; He hides to prepare. It's in His isolation that He does His best work; it's in your silence that you can hear His direction clearly. When your path feels misunderstood, allow it to be misunderstood. When you feel that you don't fit in, embrace those moments. He never created you to fit in. For the woman who thrives in solitude because God is her company, do you know how much purity lies in asking God to make your soul the most beautiful part of you? How much softness lives in thanking Him for always listening, for hearing you in moments no one else noticed, for understanding the things you could never say out loud. There is so much strength in learning that solitude is never empty when it is shared with God. That silence can become a sanctuary. That your soul was never meant to be loud to be seen, and that your softness is your biggest asset. He sees the sincerity of your heart always, and that's what matters most.

## The Art of Being Preserved– Eleni Sophia

Time doesn't heal; intention does, and that's why it's so important to be mindful of all that you do. Everything you do, touch, and speak should carry intention. Time will pass whether you choose to heal or not, but the choices you make from here are the ones aligning and shaping you into who you were meant to be. It's okay to hurt. It's okay to cry, scream, and feel lost, but in the midst of it all, I pray you never lose your faith. The woman you become after this will amaze you. God has never taken His hands off your life before, and He's not going to now. This next phase of your life is an unanswered prayer that's almost ready to unfold. You just need to show God that you're ready to trust His plan. It's okay to cry, but do you really think God would take something that was once great just to give you something worse? Never. If something or someone is removed from your life, it's often because it has run its course. He has something better, more aligned with your purpose, more fulfilling, waiting for you. He's rearranging your life, and I know the unknown feels scary, but He's never let you down before. Let Him do His work. He's bringing something far greater than what you ever had, something more aligned with His divine purpose for your life. Everything will be okay. You will be more than okay.

The Art of Being Preserved– Eleni Sophia

Never underestimate the power of a solo coffee. There is something sacred about sitting down with just yourself, no rush, no noise, no one else's voice filling the space. A simple twenty minutes can do more for your nervous system than hours of distraction ever could. It's in these small moments of peace that you begin to hear yourself again. You notice your thoughts, your feelings, the quiet whispers of your intuition. You begin to understand what you truly need, and when you understand yourself better, you naturally stop tolerating anything that doesn't honour your highest self. This is how self-respect is built. This is how clarity is restored. This is how you remember that your peace is not found in someone else's presence, but in your own. Let every sip remind you that peace was within you all along. That's the power of a solo coffee.

## The Art of Being Preserved– Eleni Sophia

She decided that she could change her life at any moment. From that point on, she became obsessed with improving herself, making herself her own passion project. By choosing herself first, she made the wisest choice: self-love. Embracing exclusivity, she understood the power of privacy, and soon nobody knew the details of her life. She learned the power of silence, perhaps the hard way, but once she grasped the luxury and strength of it, she became unrecognizable. She used her time away wisely, nurturing her soul and realizing that the entire cosmos lived within her.

## The Art of Being Preserved– Eleni Sophia

You walked away from something you believed was forever. Do you know how brave that is? You didn't just walk away; you did it with love in your heart. Do you know how Godly you are? When you choose to step away from what was never truly meant for you, you're not just letting go, you're showing the Lord how deeply you trust His plan. When you leave routine, comfort, and structure to step into the unknown, you're telling Him, 'I believe You have better for me.' That kind of faith is rare. It's powerful. Walking away from what your heart knew wasn't aligned wasn't just a decision, it was wisdom in its purest form. And do you know what you've just done? You didn't just leave; you created energetic space. Space to become a greater version of you. You cleared the path for what is truly meant for you: a love that feels like peace, for a husband whose presence feels like home. And now, you have every reason to believe that what you've been praying for is already on its way. God ended that plan because He saw it would have slowly destroyed you. You didn't lose a thing.

### The Art of Being Preserved— Eleni Sophia

Women don't only glow when they are loved well. They glow brightest when they love from their purest, untouched place. When they're unburdened by the weight of what was or what could be. It's the version of them that laughs freely, dances in the rain, and sees the world as a place full of wonder. A love without walls, where safety isn't just a feeling but a truth they can rest in. This guardless love, this safe love, is rare and transformative. It makes you want to be better. It doesn't complete them; it holds them in a way that lets their own light shine more brightly. It's the love that makes them softer, that makes their feminine energy bloom. A love that feels like home, where they are free to be imperfect, vulnerable, and fully themselves. If you're in this kind of love, may it be protected and may it last. May it remain as pure as the day it began, untouched by doubt, growing deeper with every moment shared. Because this love is a gift, not just to you, but to the world around you: a reminder of how beautiful love can be when it's rooted in safety, trust, and purity.

## The Art of Being Preserved– Eleni Sophia

If you want to know whether a woman loves herself, look at the way she treats others. Her contentment isn't just in how she holds herself, but in her quiet grace, her mannerisms, the way she moves through life. She never speaks ill of others; content women don't need to. You'll often find her in her own world, enjoying her own company, having coffee alone or dining solo. She's the nicest person in the room, yet sometimes the most envied. When she sees someone with more, she doesn't feel jealousy; she simply acknowledges how deserving that woman must be, even if she hasn't yet had her own. She doesn't tear others down; her worth isn't measured by what she lacks. And though she isn't perfect and makes mistakes like anyone else, it's who she becomes after those mistakes that sets her apart. She's an alchemist, transforming pain into growth, which is why she's so calm and content. She's mastered the art of resilience and grace, turning every setback into a step forward. A woman of faith, strength, and quiet confidence. That's how you know you've met a woman who truly values herself.

## The Art of Being Preserved– Eleni Sophia

When you meet a woman who truly values herself, you understand that no one can take what is hers. That's why she's so content. She doesn't chase, compete, or cling, because she carries a knowing in her soul. She's grasped this truth: what's meant for her will always find her. Her relationship with God is sacred, deep, and constant, and through that connection, she moves with unwavering grace and trust. She trusts the timing of her life, the path she's on, and the doors that open and close. The power of a content woman is so immense that it becomes magnetic. She lifts others effortlessly, not to prove her worth, but because she knows she is already whole. She doesn't fear lack or loss, because she's anchored in abundance. Her faith is not just something she believes; it's how she lives. That's why content women are unshakeable.

## The Art of Being Preserved – Eleni Sophia

The secret to life is living in alignment. It's listening to your intuition and becoming the best version of yourself. It's taking every setback as an opportunity to grow, even when all you want to do is stay in bed. It's doing what fulfils you, even when nobody around you understands. It's knowing you've been set apart, not in an 'I'm better than you' way, but in a way that reminds you that you were placed here for a purpose: to help others see their potential simply by walking in yours. It's going where you feel fulfilled, even if it means walking alone for a while. It's waiting for the life you know God has for you. This time is sacred. Spending it in solitude, refining yourself, is vital to align with the woman you were always meant to be. That's why understanding yourself matters. When you do, you cannot be swayed. Their opinions go in one ear and out the other. If your purpose is to spend each day discovering who you are and making the world softer and better in the process, don't let anyone who hasn't done the inner work convince you otherwise. When you live in alignment, doing what fulfils you no matter what the world thinks, that's when you've truly found yourself. If you find joy in being a homebody rather than going out, honor that. If it's learning new recipes or nurturing your home, do that. If it's climbing the corporate ladder and becoming the best at what you do, do that too. Whatever it looks like, do what brings you peace. Stop letting the noise pull you away from what your soul quietly wants. Live in alignment with who you are and never let anyone who hasn't met themselves tell you how to live your life. That's the secret to life. It's doing what feels right for your soul,

## The Art of Being Preserved– Eleni Sophia

not what looks right to others.

## The Art of Being Preserved– Eleni Sophia

Reserved and intentional women move through life differently. They've protected their inner world so deeply that they no longer mind not fitting in. Everything they do is for their future, guided by the quiet knowing that God is preparing them for something sacred. Intentional women know God will never remove their best thing, and that their decision to remain pure and disciplined today will benefit them in the long term. God fiercely protects women with discipline. The privacy of her world is her power and the place where she stays rooted. She knows who she is, what she carries, and that what is meant for her will never require her to abandon her peace. Keeping her inner state guarded and calm is her biggest priority. She knows privacy is a luxury. She doesn't need to prove anything to the world. Knowing that God is taking care of her is enough. Her contentment comes not from validation, but from her deep relationship with herself and her Creator. There is a rare kind of peace that women like you possess.

## The Art of Being Preserved— Eleni Sophia

She's *that* girl, not in an arrogant way, but in a calm, content, woman-of-faith way. The kind of woman who wants the best for everyone, even those she's had to leave behind. She wishes them healing, joy, and quiet peace, because her heart carries no bitterness. She knows she doesn't need a huge circle to live a fulfilled life. She dines alone, shops alone, drinks coffee alone, and in her own company, she blooms. Her soft heart thrives in a hard world. Every day is an opportunity for growth and fulfilment. Every setback, no matter how painful, she takes as a redirection to something greater. What's hers comes from within, so when people ask, 'How does she have all that?' or 'How is she not jealous of those who have more?' she simply knows she's co-creating with the universe. She knows she will have it all, and that knowing is rooted in wholeness. A woman of faith, she wants only to share her goodness. In a world corrupted by modern thought, she remains the embodiment of Godly values. In a world where her soul thrives when she caters. In a world where all she does is Pilates, drink solo coffee, challenge her mind, shop, and pray, she is the softness this world needs. She is whole and complete on her own, but when she's loved right, she becomes a woman even God smiles upon: nurturing, radiant, and the peace every king prays for.

### The Art of Being Preserved– Eleni Sophia

When you know and understand yourself fully, you cannot and do not settle. Not in love, not in friendships, not in the company you keep. A woman who knows her worth is not accessible to everyone. When she walks with God, she doesn't fear being hated or misunderstood, because she was never created for the approval of the crowd. Her circle is often just herself, and with every solo date she discovers more of what lies in her heart. Being told 'you have no friends' becomes one of the greatest compliments because it shows she needs no one outside herself to feel whole. She stays in constant conversation with God, and it is there that she finds her worth, her peace, and her power.

The Art of Being Preserved— Eleni Sophia

## Returning Home

To the girl in the weird in-between feeling of heartbreak and peace, that's your soul returning home to itself. For years you've lived on an edge, in survival, waiting for the next moment to fall apart. It's time to let your nervous system reset. Let morning be enough. Let slowness be sacred. You don't have to prove that you're okay. You don't have to rush your healing. Take each day as it comes. The ache you feel now isn't weakness, it's release. It's everything you once held in finally having space to leave your body. And it's safe to let it go. Most importantly, forgive yourself. Every time you stayed too long, every time you silenced yourself to keep the peace, every time you put someone else's comfort above your own, it wasn't for nothing. It softened you in the right places. It gave you the wisdom you'll need for what's ahead. It was all practice, so when true love arrives, you recognize it with healed eyes and a healed heart. You're not starting over; you're starting from wholeness. You're not behind; you're on divine timing. You're moving from self-trust, from a deeper knowing that love doesn't have to hurt to be real. And next time, you won't lose yourself trying to be chosen. You'll already know that you are.

## The Art of Being Preserved– Eleni Sophia

The sacred power of being allows you to rest in His company. There is a quiet strength that comes from no longer needing to prove, chase, or perform. It's the kind of power that sits beneath the surface: calm, certain, and anchored in faith. The sacred power of being is about remembering who you are before the world told you to become more. It's where peace replaces pressure, where alignment replaces effort, and where softness becomes your shield. It's when you're known for the boldness of your faith. It's understanding that access to you is sacred; it's not that you dislike everyone; you've simply developed a low tolerance for those who no longer add value to your being. It's knowing that prayer is communication with God, and solitude is where you begin to hear His direction. It's living a life where you've mastered detachment. You no longer prove yourself or seek validation from the external. You live through the art of simply being. When someone says something untrue, instead of defense, a simple 'okay' is enough. It's knowing who you are even when deeply misunderstood by the world. So, continue being someone who does the inner work, find home within yourself. Solitude isn't always comfortable, but it is sacred. The universe is never wrong in its mathematics. Inner work will *always* be repaid. Godly women carry a calm that does not need to be proven; they know there is power in stillness with Him. Every calling begins with separation. This period of separation is where peace is reborn, and clarity is restored. Become still enough to feel God breathing through your simple art of being. Devote time to self-purification and let

## The Art of Being Preserved— Eleni Sophia

nothing enter your inner world without alignment.

### The Art of Being Preserved— Eleni Sophia

Slow down. Breathe. The world is quietly holding you. Walk through life knowing there is goodness in everything. The power of awareness begins with knowing yourself. When you slow down enough to meet your own presence, you start to notice how connected everything really is. Human connection isn't always loud or obvious; sometimes it's as simple as someone sitting beside you in a coffee shop to have their lunch. You shared a moment with them, even in silence. You were never alone; you were just unaware. We often move through our days so quickly that we forget to see the world that's quietly holding us. The way the sunlight hits the window and keeps you warm. The warmth of your coffee cup between your hands. The hum of life around you. These are all reminders that you are a part of something much bigger, something soft and sacred. Take a moment today to put your phone down. To breathe. To walk in your own presence. To notice the small miracles that exist without asking for your attention. The more you slow down, the more you realize life has always been this beautiful: you just had to be still enough to see it.

## The Art of Being Preserved— Eleni Sophia

Go inwards. Find yourself. Discover who you are. Hide if you need to, but whatever you do, do it with intention. Take this hibernation as a sacred opportunity to become a better you. I know you're hurting, and maybe you're still holding onto resentment, but when you take each day as it comes, you naturally begin to detach from what was never meant for you. In time, even just a few months, you'll see why things had to happen this way. Go somewhere nobody knows you or your story and give yourself the space to simply *become*. When you go inward, you heal in ways you can't always see yet. When you disappear quietly and devote that time to yourself, you start to notice truths, patterns, and possibilities you once ignored. You meet yourself in a new light. When you step outside your comfort zone and try new things, you uncover a version of you that's always existed but never had room to breathe. There is a version of you that deserves to be seen, but only by you first.

## The Art of Being Preserved— Eleni Sophia

Most importantly, keep your progress between you and your Creator. This is your sacred season. See it as a hibernation of the soul. Let the world move on without you for a while. Immerse yourself in becoming, not for applause or an outcome, but for alignment. This is *your* season, and the right people will still be there when you return. The wrong ones won't. Either way, you'll be okay. This is the part no one sees: the unbecoming, the unlearning, the slowing down to meet yourself where you are, without judgement, without rush. And I promise you, when you go inward, truly inward, you'll begin to heal in places you didn't even know were broken. You'll remember truths you forgot. You'll gather the pieces you abandoned just to survive. And what rises from this quiet becoming is the woman you've always been, but never fully met. Please don't overshare this journey with people who won't understand it, especially not with those who don't live the kind of life you're trying to build. Honor every solo coffee. Every journal entry. Every silent prayer. And remember: God will never take your best thing.

## The Art of Being Preserved— Eleni Sophia

She's coming back home to herself by going inward. Not seeking answers from the outside world, not looking for approval, just returning to her quiet truth. She's peeling back layers that were never hers to carry. She's releasing. She's reconnecting with the woman she was always meant to be soft, sacred, and deeply led by faith. She's not becoming someone new; she's coming home to herself. Her nervous system is resetting. She's shedding old versions, old desires, old timelines she thought she had to follow. And God was with her every step of the way. She asked Him to heal her, and He heard. He always hears. He may not answer how you imagined, but He always answers. Sometimes in silence, sometimes through redirection, sometimes by closing doors you were never meant to open. But always in ways that gently realign you with the path meant for you. The path that leads to your highest, truest, most whole self.

She's coming back home to herself.

### The Art of Being Preserved– Eleni Sophia

Don't ask what happened to her. God took care of her. She didn't post a soft launch or announce her glow-up. There was no dramatic exit, no curated comeback, no need to be seen. She just disappeared, quietly and completely, because that's how real healing begins. He pulled her away from people who couldn't appreciate her softness, from environments that dimmed her light, from cycles she didn't even realize she was repeating. She didn't cut people off; she simply outgrew what wasn't good for her higher self. She became softer, quieter, wiser, because God taught her how to be whole without being seen. She no longer needed to prove she was okay; she just *was*. And now she's at peace with being the girl who disappeared. The one no one can quite place or label. Because the truth is, she ended up with herself. She ended up with peace. She ended up with God. So don't ask what happened to her. Just know:
God is her companion, and she's never going back.

## The Art of Being Preserved— Eleni Sophia

A message to the pure woman navigating heartbreak. I know you're hurting, but I also know you understand how deeply God loves you. You've seen His protection time and time again, in ways that only made sense later. He wouldn't have removed this from your life unless He knew it no longer served your soul. Once you truly believe that God never removes without the intention to replace with better, life begins to feel softer. You start to see that the pain you're feeling isn't just necessary, it's sacred. It's shaping you into the woman you're meant to be for the next phase of your life. Life moves in phases. It's transitional. The woman you're becoming has outgrown the love she once thought she needed. She's calling in a different kind of love now, something deeper, wiser, more grounded in true masculine energy. It's not that the giddiness and romance won't exist; it's that this new love will meet you where you are, in alignment with who you've become. This is a rebirth into an evolved self. The evolved you is learning that every day is a chance to grow, every moment is a chance to pause and say, 'I don't like this. I'm going to shift this.' They say it takes ninety days to change a habit, but with intention and faith, transformation can begin in just a few. Your higher self can move towards you faster than you think.

### The Art of Being Preserved— Eleni Sophia

It's hard to keep pouring into others when you have nothing left within yourself. So, from now on, I want you to choose yourself. And in choosing yourself, I want you to go all in. Please don't seek validation from the outside world. You need to go all in on you. Ultimately, you're the only person who will be with you 100% of the time. This isn't a call to stop loving the world; it's a reminder not to let the world harden the purity within you. Nurture your well-being, and from that place of wholeness, you'll continue to pour beautiful love into the world. When you allow God to guide you again, you'll slowly uncover the best version of yourself, radiating a softness and light that are entirely yours. Remember, it's okay to take all the time you need to find yourself again. The journey back to self-discovery and realignment is a beautiful one.

## The Art of Being Preserved— Eleni Sophia

A solitary path is far more rewarding than one where you have to beg to be seen or constantly prove your worth. Walking alone can feel quiet at first, but if you allow it, it will teach you. It will show you how to stand firm in who you are without needing validation. This season will transform you. It will stretch you, soften you, and strengthen your soul in ways you never expected. When you walk alone with God, you begin to understand that solitude isn't punishment, it's preparation. It's where you learn that peace is better than attention, alignment is better than approval, and not everyone is meant to walk beside you. The solitary path is sacred because it leads you back home to yourself, where your worth always lived.

### The Art of Being Preserved— Eleni Sophia

Whilst the rest of the world fights to be seen, chasing validation and temporary highs, you don't think God sees you? Every time you choose to seclude yourself so you can pour into your future and become the best version of you, He sees you. Every time you sit alone instead of joining conversations that don't serve your highest good, He sees you. This season of preparation will never go to waste. It may take time to show, but when it does, it will be one of the most sacred unions, created in the eyes of God. A woman who walks with this level of *knowing* in His plan will always come out on top. She will be used as a living demonstration of the power of walking through life with this much faith.

### The Art of Being Preserved— Eleni Sophia

Your external world will always mirror your inner world. When you choose to create peace within your mind, it will show in your life. You are such a rare entity. With intentions as pure as yours, of course God is going to give you the best. He is simply testing to see whether you will stay true to yourself.

### The Art of Being Preserved— Eleni Sophia

Your inability to think for yourself is what will land you in trouble in the long term, because God loves to test people's faith when everyone around them is trying to convince them of something that, deep down, they know isn't right for the season they're in. That's why oneness within yourself matters so much. There is power in knowing yourself, in spending time alone, in understanding your purpose, and in trusting His plan for you. He is always watching to see whether you will give in to the life others want for you or stay true to your intuition and do what's best for your soul. What is meant for you can never miss you - never. There is no need to try and speed it up. As humans, we're so used to believing we must control everything, when the truth is that His timing is the only timing. So please, know yourself, trust yourself, and remember: He always has your best interests at heart - more than anyone.

## The Art of Being Preserved– Eleni Sophia

If your heart is pure and your intentions are honest, if your mission each day is to make your soul your most beautiful feature, then why are you worried? He's already written the ending, and it's better than anything you're praying for. He's always had your best interest at heart. Become the best you, and He will handle the rest.

## The Art of Being Preserved— Eleni Sophia

Just know, when you're not interested in being loud, hard, or competitive, and it still triggers people, it means you're doing something right. They'll always have something to say when your softness brings you peace, protection, and provision. When your days are spent doing what you love in your own company, when your focus is your mind, your body, and your soul, when you're building a home instead of chasing a hustle, when you're becoming the woman you prayed to be, it will still bother them. When you are a woman of grace and authenticity, a woman who keeps to herself, minds her own business, and works quietly on becoming better each day, don't be surprised when those who don't share your values have something to say. You can be the kindest woman in the world, live as softly and sacredly as you choose, and people will still talk. Let them. Softness is still your power. Peace is still your priority. Becoming *her* is still your mission.

## The Art of Being Preserved– Eleni Sophia

She learned that peace arrived when she protected her kingdom. From the moment she prioritized herself, there was no turning back. Despite the negativity from small minds trying to distort her calm, her resilience always prevailed. She may have looked like she 'failed' to some, but she simply withdrew her energy from others and invested it into herself. Each day became a chance for self-nurturing, for feeding her mind and body with what made her stronger, and for mastering her thoughts. She finally understood she was the only one in control of her feelings; no external force could touch her peace unless she let it. Once she protected her home, she protected her mind, and once that became clear, beautiful things began to manifest with ease. The moment she decided to put herself first, there was no going back. That's the thing about self-love; once you begin, you don't return to who you were before. With each passing day, she fell more in love with the woman she was becoming.

### The Art of Being Preserved– Eleni Sophia

When the feeling of 'God, make me for more than this' comes out of nowhere, I hope you don't ignore it. That's not random; it's a holy reminder. I hope you find the courage to pause. Not to escape your life, but to redesign it. I hope you reconnect with your highest self, the version of you led by her intuition and her own mind, not by the noise of the world. Soft but sure. Quiet but called. I hope you make time to pray, not from fear, but to hear the next instruction. He's always in communication with you; this is why self-awareness and mindfulness are so important. If that whisper came to you, believe it. It was never a question. It was a reminder.

### The Art of Being Preserved– Eleni Sophia

And as you sit in your stillness and recognise the power in your solitude, I pray you understand how capable you are. How whole and complete you are. How wonderful you are. How soft you are. I pray you understand how truly marvellous you are. How your intentions are pure. How everything you do is laced with love. How your presence makes the world pause in quiet awe. I pray you understand the power you hold. I pray you never lose sight of how incredible you are. I pray you have it all. Your ability to inspire awe is powerful. Know the power you possess and never forget your worth. You have everything you need to create a life that fulfils you, and God's timing is perfect.

## The Art of Being Preserved— Eleni Sophia

Do you know how beautiful it is to stay true to yourself when the whole world tells you to get into a relationship or just find someone? But you trust God's timing. Those are the women He rewards the most. I hope you know you're not behind. You're exactly where God needs you to be. You've never been in a relationship? Good. That doesn't make you less; it makes you preserved.

We live in a generation obsessed with comparison, where people treat past relationships like trophies. But God never called you to live comparatively. He created you in His image, not as a reflection of your peers. So, when others try to push you into things that don't align with your path, there is so much power in staying true to yourself, even if it means sitting alone at most tables.

In a world where it's considered a 'flex' to have many, I hope you realize how rare and beautiful it is that you remain true. True to yourself, to your values, and to the quiet promises you've made with God. You are exactly where you need to be. And what's yours will never miss you.

## Becoming *Her*

The reward after hardship is the *becoming*. It's aligning with a version of yourself you once believed was out of reach. A version your younger self would feel safe around. A version she would look at with admiration and think, I hope I grow into someone like her. A woman who chose healing even when it was heavy, who kept her softness even after being hurt, who kept promises to herself and showed up for herself even on days she was tired and felt unseen. Who carries strength not loud or forceful, but steady and sure. That is the reward: becoming the woman you needed, the woman you were always meant to be. So yes, after hardship, there is always reward.

## The Art of Being Preserved— Eleni Sophia

I'm trying to find the balance between taking the little girl inside me out of her comfort zone and helping her grow, while also reminding her it's okay to slow down and take care of her soul. It's okay to take time to understand what you need. It's okay to breathe and not be so hard on yourself. Rediscovering the softest version of you isn't always easy, especially if you've been living in a certain dynamic for years. But I want you to trust that things are unfolding exactly as they should. Finding balance between mourning what once was, embracing change, and stepping into a new version of yourself will feel unpredictable at times. Still, it's within this messiness that you rediscover who you are at your core. That's when you remember your softness. Your authenticity. Your truth. See this as a rejuvenating retreat rather than a loss. It's a transition into a higher version of yourself. And through it, you come out stronger, more open, and more aligned with the woman you've always been destined to be. Everything you do, do it mindfully. I know you're hurting. You're mourning, whether it's the loss of someone else or the girl you used to be. You deserve a life that feels gentle. Things will fall into place.

## The Art of Being Preserved— Eleni Sophia

Big sister advice? It's much better to be the one who got away, the one wrapped in mystery, the one nobody can quite explain, than the one who was chosen too soon, before her becoming was complete. God is giving you the rarest gift: space to transform, to grow, to rise into the woman you were always meant to be. Do you know how much of a blessing that is? Your entire life is a blessing. Every delay, every redirection, every unanswered question is an invitation to trust Him more deeply. And the more you trust Him, the more He blesses you. Life is a journey. It's not meant to be rushed or compared but lived with God by your side. When you move through life consciously like this, walking with grace, believing everything is working out for you, you become a magnet for greatness. And you, my dear, were always destined for the best.

## The Art of Being Preserved— Eleni Sophia

She's good. And she's always going to be good. Because when your spirit is pure and your heart is light, God keeps extra hands on you, guiding, covering, correcting gently, and placing you exactly where you need to be, even when you don't understand why. When you're a woman so deeply rooted in trust and divinity, God cherishes you differently. A woman of this calibre may face more challenges, but deep down she knows it's for her growth. It's for her becoming. She's not lucky, she's aligned. She moves with ease because she trusts in something bigger than herself. She doesn't have to fight for clarity; it follows her. A woman that soft, that surrendered, that rooted in God is divinely protected. He doesn't let her fall too far. Not now. Not ever. Because He always keeps extra hands on a woman like her.

## The Art of Being Preserved– Eleni Sophia

Chosen women walk alone. Not because they want to, but because they've been set apart by their Lord for more. When God has a bigger calling for you, He pulls you away from the noise. He protects you. He trains you in secret. Your path won't look like anyone else's, and it's not supposed to. The world won't get it; you'll probably be deeply misunderstood and that's okay. A union with God forms when you stop judging, stop competing, stop looking left and right, and become whole within yourself. When your energy is high and clean because you're focused only on becoming a better version of who He made you to be. Your eyes stay on Him. You lean on His guidance for every step. And yes, distractions will come. People will try to pull you off your path. But a woman of God knows when to stay grounded. She knows what He's asked of her, and she's not willing to lose that for anyone. Her only goal is to be the kind of woman God is proud of. So, she may walk alone, but never without Him.

## The Art of Being Preserved– Eleni Sophia

A message to the good woman. Never forget the magnetic woman that you are. Never forget the quiet power that moves through you. The thing about pure women, pure in intention and pure at the very core of their heart, is that their connection to their Creator runs deeper than anything in this world. It's constant, it's quiet, it's unbreakable. An intentional woman moves differently because she's guided by something higher. The opinions of others don't sway her; she's led by God and her intuition only. It doesn't matter if the entire world is doing something, if she knows it's not beneficial for her higher good, she will simply step away. She's not boring; her future family is constantly on her mind. Even if she's been mistreated, she'll wish them the best and move away with love in her heart. She can see another woman winning, being loved, being celebrated, and it does not make her bitter. It makes her hopeful. It makes her pray even harder for the promises over her own life. Godly women do not complain. They do not scheme, and they definitely don't plot or gossip. When something unsettles her spirit, she speaks to Him. She takes her worries to Him and Him alone. Her circle is small. Most days it is just her and God, and that's always been enough.

### The Art of Being Preserved– Eleni Sophia

A Godly woman does not demand attention; she doesn't even want it anymore. She moves in silence, embracing each day as an opportunity for growth. To the world, she's disappeared, but in reality, she is in an era of *feeling* rather than being seen. Her life is not up for public consumption. She does not chase status for validation but rises for the life she has chosen so she can serve and nurture in the best way possible. That is her true femininity: her ability to care, protect, and uplift, even those she does not know. Every day is a chance for self-development. She competes with no one. There is no need for her to be loud, to share her every move, or to seek approval from the world. This woman has evolved from wanting to take over the world to no longer needing to be seen. She has reached a level of contentment that many crave.
A Godly woman understands this at her very core.

## The Art of Being Preserved– Eleni Sophia

Content women walk with God because they know they're always covered. They see someone who has a life they desire and instead of feeling envious, they see her as an inspiration. There's a certain refinement to women who live this way, a beauty in the ones who clap for others, who turn another woman's blessing into motivation instead of bitterness. A woman truly aligned with God knows His abundance is eternal. He adores those who put their entire trust in Him. If you want to know if a woman truly values herself, look at the way she treats others. Her contentment isn't just in how she holds herself but in her quiet grace, her manners, and the way she navigates life. She never speaks ill of others; content women don't need to. You'll often find her in her own world, enjoying her own company, having coffee alone or dining solo. When she sees someone with more, she doesn't feel jealousy; she simply acknowledges how deserving that woman must be, even if she hasn't yet had her own. She doesn't tear others down; her worth isn't measured by what she lacks. And though she isn't perfect and makes mistakes like anyone else, it's who she becomes after those mistakes that sets her apart. She's an alchemist, forever transforming pain into growth.

## The Art of Being Preserved— Eleni Sophia

A content woman knows that what is hers can never be taken away. She knows another woman's answered prayer is not a threat, but a reminder that her own prayers are also heard.

## The Art of Being Preserved– Eleni Sophia

She's fearless because of her faith. Making her heart the purest thing about her is her biggest priority. When you focus on the condition of your heart and have genuine intentions for those around you, life has a way of working out. But a Godly life isn't always soft; it requires discipline. It means showing Him that you trust His plan, even when you have no idea why things are unfolding the way they are. That's where faith lives. Not when it all makes sense, but when it doesn't and you *still* choose Him. It takes talking to God daily and choosing a path that He's pleased with. Understanding He is the One entity that will never leave your side. He is your provider, protector, nourisher; He has always shown up, even when you forgot Him. Detaching from the worldly life of attention and validation becomes her priority. When you sit in prayer and ask God to make your soul the purest thing about you, He always hears you. She's fearless because of her faith.

## The Art of Being Preserved— Eleni Sophia

You must allow yourself to be loved. You may have had a painful experience before, but things are different now. Look at you. You see your flaws for what they are, and you understand they make you imperfectly perfect. You cherish yourself differently now. You feel happier in your own skin. Do not let the past change your view of love. If this next love isn't the one, you will not fall apart the way you once did, because you have yourself now. Your healing has made you stronger, steadier, safer within your own soul. You are whole, with or without anyone. But still, allow yourself to experience love. Things are different now. You have you.

### The Art of Being Preserved— Eleni Sophia

Never let anyone tell you how to live your life, whether their intentions are pure or impure. Always listen to your own heart. It is there that God whispers the loudest.

That is the power of a woman who knows herself. The power of a woman who honors her boundaries, who protects her home, and who refuses to let anyone disrupt the peace she's built. A woman who knows herself fully, completely, and wholly is a woman God continues to elevate. She will be misunderstood. She will be tested, often through people who think they know what's best for her. But when she knows herself, and when she rests in God's timing, everything flows for her. Look at her life and you'll see why she's so peaceful. She has more peace than anyone you know. Why? Because she trusts Him. Why? Because she knows herself.

### The Art of Being Preserved— Eleni Sophia

To the woman who has spent most of her life in solitude because she's been misunderstood or simply couldn't find people who align with her values, just know it will all pay off. You haven't lowered your boundaries for anybody, do you know how powerful you are? The promises kept between you and your Creator are sacred and so are you. In a world where it's the norm to speak down on your partner, you protect yours with prayer. Your prayers have shielded him for years. You keep your business between you and the one who created you. You don't overshare; you know there's no need. And that's why you haven't found your people. That's why it's been so difficult for you to fit in. This is your reminder that life is going to work out for you in more ways than you can imagine. To the woman who's been misunderstood her whole life, you shouldn't be sad; you've kept to your morals despite being in a world obsessed with temptation. Women like you were not made to fit in rooms with ordinary people. When you step into a room you don't even need to say a word for them to notice your magnetism. You're not behind and you're not missing out. You're in your *becoming* era, an intentional season where you're learning yourself, choosing yourself, and letting God lead. And when the right people and opportunities come, you won't have to perform or pretend. Your presence will speak for itself. You were never meant to blend in; women like you were always meant to shine.

## The Art of Being Preserved– Eleni Sophia

You have no idea how sacred you are. Your presence alone moves rooms. Your energy, your essence, it carries weight. It speaks before you do. Never stop working on yourself, because you are your greatest asset. And as you grow, I pray you do it with deep intention. May every aspect of your body, mind, and soul feel the awareness and care you bring toward it. You are not just evolving; you are returning to the purest version of yourself. At the very essence of her soul lay purity. A heart so content, even if she hadn't yet achieved all her dreams. Because she knew gratitude, presence, and joy for others were her greatest strengths. She never resented the success of those around her. Instead, she clapped, cheered, and remained unwavering in her own journey, knowing her manifestations were on the way. And no matter what she faced, she never neglected her higher self. And she never lost faith in Him. No matter how cruel the world could be, she always returned to the kind-hearted woman within her. I hope you never forget her.

## The Art of Being Preserved– Eleni Sophia

Just her and her alone time against the world. She learned to cherish her own company, knowing that 'table for one, please' wasn't a sign of loneliness, but of peace. God was within her, and in her solitude, she found clarity and strength. She walked away from anything that didn't help her thrive, valuing mindfulness and presence over encounters that no longer served her. Alone, she discovered the true meaning of self-love and realized she didn't need anyone to complete her; she was already whole. In those quiet moments, with every sip of coffee she enjoyed alone, with every Pilates class she showed up to for herself, she uncovered the beauty of her own company. She realized that 'table for one, please' wasn't just an act of independence; it was a declaration of peace. God was always with her, guiding her through every step of her journey. With every act of self-care, she found clarity. With every boundary she set, she found strength. She left behind what no longer helped her thrive, choosing instead to pour into herself. She didn't need anyone to complete her; she became whole on her own. In her solitude, she unlocked the power of self-belief, determination, and grace. And in those moments, she truly began to shine.

## The Art of Being Preserved— Eleni Sophia

I know you're hurting, but this is your reminder that God is never taking His hands off you. Especially when you're a woman whose faith is strong, whose heart is pure, who smiles at strangers without expecting anything in return. The woman who sees someone praying and quietly prays their wish comes true. The one who wishes the best for everyone, even those who received what she once cried for. Do you really believe God would place such a deep desire in your heart only to leave it unfinished? During these seasons of pain, isolation, and transformation, that's when He does His most careful work. He hasn't forgotten you. Even in the moments where you feel behind or overlooked, He is refining you. He's teaching you how to be whole without needing to be seen. He's protecting your softness, reminding you that rare hearts like yours are not meant to be easily accessed. Let Him do His best work in you, especially on days you think otherwise. You are safe in this becoming.

### The Art of Being Preserved— Eleni Sophia

Women like you were made with rare gentleness in a world that celebrates hardness. That softness is not something you need to grow out of, even if you've never met anyone with the same individuality. Especially so. Your life is proof that you were intentionally created by a careful, loving Creator. I hope you know it's okay to live a life that doesn't make sense to them. I hope you never lower your standards just to fit in or belong to a group that was never built to hold someone like you. When God created you, do you really think He made you to fit in? Do you believe He wanted you lost in the noise or swept into the chaos? Absolutely not. He formed you for calm. For clarity. For something quieter, something sacred. He made you with divine care and so much intention; you can feel it. Others can feel it. Strangers sense it before you even speak. It's in the way you move through the world with grace, not force. In the way your words land gently, even when they're few. In your wisdom to keep sacred things sacred, to share with the best listener instead of people. When a woman's life is ordained by God, she lets Him lead. Her only job is to remain soft, stay close to Him and trust the timing of His plan.

## The Art of Being Preserved— Eleni Sophia

The reality of being a Godly woman takes discipline and clarity of the heart. It takes a deep trust and understanding that this world is temporary, nothing in this world belongs to us. The best plans for your life are His plans. And when you walk through life with this innate knowing that in every moment, He always has your best interest at heart, life just has a way of working out for you.

### The Art of Being Preserved– Eleni Sophia

When you're a good woman in an overstimulated environment, it's hard to admit you need space. You tell yourself everything is fine, and you'll eventually come into alignment, but how can you find yourself in the same space you lost yourself in? And it's okay to feel that way. Everything happening in your life is shaping your soul in the way it's meant to. It's in your nature to give, to nurture, to love effortlessly. So, when you no longer recognize yourself in those traits, you feel disconnected from your purpose. You love deeply but often feel disappointed by the lack of reciprocation. Months later, you realize you've lost yourself, stuck between pouring from an empty cup and wanting to live in your purpose by expressing the most genuine love from your highest, most feminine self. When you don't feel protected or held by grounded masculine energy, you start protecting yourself. Inevitably, your masculine begins to rise. You've always been a woman of faith, so God has always given you the tools to thrive, but when you stay in an environment that keeps you overstimulated and, in your masculine, it becomes difficult to live through your true purpose. It's okay to make space for yourself.

## The Art of Being Preserved— Eleni Sophia

You're not saying goodbye to love. You're saying goodbye to the version of love that asked you to abandon yourself just to feel seen. You're not grieving what you lost externally; you're grieving the part of you that once gave everything just to be understood. You were soft, loyal, and pure. You gave the best of you. But this next chapter belongs to the woman who no longer needs to be remembered to feel lovable. It's for the version of you who will thrive in her own light, who knows that real love will never require her to shrink, chase, or prove. It will meet her where she stands: whole, grounded, and at peace within herself.

## The Art of Being Preserved— Eleni Sophia

Take nothing personally; understand how others treat you is simply projection. Once you've mastered the art of understanding how precious your life is, you'll stop allowing the opinions and treatment from others to affect the rest of your day. This is a skill that can take years to master, but once you stop allowing the external world to disrupt your inner peace, you set yourself free. True freedom begins when you realize that you are not a reflection of someone else's insecurities or judgments. You are such a unique girl with grace and dignity, and no one has the power to dim that light unless you allow it. Your time and energy are sacred and wasting them on overanalyzing others' actions or opinions is not an option in the life of a Godly woman, especially if they're the actions of those who aren't whole and content in themselves.

### The Art of Being Preserved– Eleni Sophia

A good woman, a woman of value, has what she has because her Creator sees her as worthy enough to sustain all the luxuries in life and more. Her Lord recognizes all her great qualities and rewards her accordingly. Just because her goodness couldn't be appreciated by some, it doesn't mean it's not by the rest of the world. God sees her as powerful enough to be the queen of her home, a man's best asset. If others can't find that love within themselves, it doesn't give them the right to try and take it from a woman who is truly deserving of all the wonderful things life has to offer.

The Art of Being Preserved— Eleni Sophia

And as you align with the woman you were always meant to be, I hope you find the strength to become a woman who knows herself so fully that she never allows the opinions of outsiders to interfere with what she knows God has prepared for her. A woman who is in tune with herself and her intuition trusts in God's timing and in the life He has designed for her. When she moves through life with this awareness, everything begins to align and unfolds for the betterment of her highest self.

## The Art of Being Preserved– Eleni Sophia

And so, she remembered who she was. It's easy to forget your values, your beliefs, and boundaries when you've been in situations that made you feel like you had to shrink to be accepted. I hope you never forget the woman who lives at the heart of your being. You were never meant to stay in places that made you feel small. Maybe you were meant to pass through them for a while, long enough to remember who you are, but they were never your forever. Any friendship, place, or family dynamic that left you out, dismissed your presence, or laughed at your politeness was never your home. You've been in survival mode for too long and now it's a chance for your nervous system to reset. Please remember, healing looks different for everybody. Sometimes it's crying, releasing, or purging everything you've been holding in. Other times, it's going to Pilates, drinking your matcha, trying new things, or sitting quietly with yourself and simply being. It might mean reading a good book, praying, or spending long moments in solitude. Whatever form it takes for you, I want you to know that your healing is valid, even if it doesn't look like anyone else's. You are still evolving, still becoming, even in the stillness. God has written such a unique story for you, which means your journey cannot be compared. Trust your intuition on how to move through this phase. Go inward. Sit with yourself. Meditate. Remember the girl who lies at your core and spend time in prayer asking God to align you with your highest self.

## The Art of Being Preserved– Eleni Sophia

When you've built an inner world of peace, protect the frequency that keeps you sane. Energetic boundary fatigue is real. It's what happens when you're doing everything right on the outside, spending time alone, choosing peace, minding your business, yet one conversation with someone leaves you drained because of how much emotional noise you had to filter. You spend a few hours with someone and think never again. That's not coldness, it's clarity. It's knowing you've worked too hard to protect your inner world. It's not arrogance, it's your higher self speaking to you. Your energy is too expensive for chaos. When you're God's girl, you live knowing everything is working out for your highest good. So, when others project their pain or limiting beliefs and your body quietly rejects it, that's your sign to step away. If you have dinner with someone and go home feeling drained, it's okay to protect yourself.

### The Art of Being Preserved– Eleni Sophia

We live in a world where instead of people talking to God, they run to people. If someone no longer aligns with where you see yourself in five years, it's okay to let go. There is so much importance in protecting your inner world. You really are the sum of the five people you spend the most time with, and if you haven't found your group yet, know this: there's far more power in solitude than in forced connection. Access to you is expensive. Rejuvenate your mind from any energy that doesn't serve your highest good. Don't seek comfort in those who don't even value themselves. Your path is sacred; protect it like the precious gem it is. Trust yourself, and when you need guidance, turn inward. God gave you intuition for a reason, please listen to it. When you're pure, when you've freed yourself from other people's limiting mindsets, you liberate yourself. They'll call it detachment or delusion, but you'll know the truth; it's trust. It's trusting God's plan so deeply that you no longer question if it's working out, you know it already is.

## The Art of Being Preserved— Eleni Sophia

The woman you are becoming requires peace more than attention; she requires silence more than validation. She's learning that privacy is her greatest luxury and discipline her softest form of self-love. She no longer explains her growth; she embodies it. She no longer seeks to be understood; she's too focused on becoming who God called her to be.
This one's for the woman in her *becoming*.

## The Art of Being Preserved— Eleni Sophia

It is a special kind of emptiness and bitterness to try and tear down a woman who stands whole and secure within herself, simply because they haven't found that same love or peace within their own soul. When they're consumed by their own insecurities and self-doubt, it's easy to feel threatened by someone who radiates confidence and self-assuredness. Her strength, her completeness, becomes a mirror reflecting everything they feel they lack, and instead of facing that inner void, they attempt to bring her down to their level. But what they fail to realize is that her wholeness is not dependent on their validation or approval. Her sense of self isn't something they can take away, no matter how much bitterness they carry. She's done the work to build herself up from within, to fill her own cup. So, their attempts to diminish her will only reveal more about their own insecurities than anything about her. Most importantly, it'll be worse for them when they see they've failed in their attempt to bring her down because of how close she is to God. It's not her they are battling; it's the parts of themselves that they refuse to confront. If only they would turn inward, they'd see that tearing others down doesn't bring peace; it only perpetuates the cycle of emptiness. The real strength lies not in attacking others but in healing themselves.

## The Art of Being Preserved— Eleni Sophia

One day, you'll truly understand what sacred love is. A man will enter your life in the most unexpected way. The moment he sees you, he'll recognize the precious gem that you are. His eyes will be for you alone, and he'll be determined to show you the true meaning of love. He'll never understand how anyone could ever hurt someone as precious as you, and he'll make it his mission to fulfil your needs. You'll never have to beg this man for anything. You'll never sit with a lump in your throat wondering whether he'll show up for you. You'll feel excitement again. By then, you'll already be content alone, but this man's purpose will be to show you that you don't have to carry everything alone. He will see you for the soft, delicate soul that you are and cherish you like the invaluable treasure you've always been. He'll put you first, unafraid to disregard other people's opinions if it means protecting you. You'll wonder where he's been your whole life, and you'll spend the rest of your life thanking God for him. For now, continue to grow back into the soft, gentle woman you once were. The world is waiting to see that side of you again. Not the one that answers every question with, 'I don't know.' It won't be an easy journey, but you will rediscover what it feels like to be soft again.

The Art of Being Preserved— Eleni Sophia

One day you'll wake up and realize God never took anything from you. He saw what you couldn't, heard what you didn't, and simply said, 'not with my girl.'

The Art of Being Preserved– Eleni Sophia

## The power in knowing yourself

There is an innate power in choosing yourself every day. Not the version expected of you, because your life was never meant to be understood by everybody, but the version God called you to be. The more you lean into who God created you to be, the freer you become. You stop living for approval and start living in alignment. You stop apologizing for your light and start walking in it fully. When you choose yourself, the world loses its power to shake you, because your heart learns to rest in who you truly are. And with every small choosing, with every decision to put yourself first, your bond with your Creator grows softer, stronger, unshakable.

When you choose yourself, nothing anyone says can sway you. Your heart rests in who you truly are. And as your bond with God deepens, you begin to trust His plan for you even more. God already knows who you are, He knows what lays in your heart and it's time you understand yourself. Life is a journey of trials and tribulations meant to align us with who we were always destined to be. And when you've taken the time to know yourself and trust Him, you see that tribulations aren't here to destroy you but to grow you. We already know God never burdens a soul with pain beyond its capacity. That doesn't mean the path is easy, but it does mean you walk it with knowing, with faith that all will be well, with clarity that every step is shaping you into the woman you were born to become.

## The Art of Being Preserved— Eleni Sophia

There is an art in understanding who you are and once you've taken the time to truly know yourself, you've mastered an art many crave in this lifetime. Taking yourself on a solo date becomes more than self-care. It's a way of meeting yourself, uninterrupted, unbothered by the outside world. It's how you remind yourself that even if you stand alone, you will always be okay, because you and God are enough.

The Art of Being Preserved– Eleni Sophia

The best growth happens when you surrender to God's calling, when you trust His plans above your own. Because when God is your bestie, you are never alone.

## The Art of Being Preserved– Eleni Sophia

Life bends for the woman who knows God has her back. She doesn't rush. She moves like she's protected, because she is. She knows what's meant for her will never need chasing. When she's grounded in God, doors open naturally. Her rest is worship. Her silence is trust. Everything she desires is always making its way to her. Because life always bends for the woman who walks with God.

### The Art of Being Preserved— Eleni Sophia

You won't always understand why God isolates you before He elevates you. But isolation is protection. It's pruning. It's preparation. When everything around you feels like it's falling apart, trust that something deeper is falling into place. He is removing the noise so you can hear Him clearly. He is redirecting you toward the life He wrote for you long before you learned to pray for it. You are not behind. You're not late. You're being aligned.

## The Art of Being Preserved— Eleni Sophia

The woman who knows that loneliness and solitude are not the same understands her own power. Loneliness is what you feel when you have drifted away from yourself; solitude is what you feel when you have come home to her. It is in that sacred quiet, in that stillness with God, that she grows, heals, and remembers who she was always meant to be. At the end of it all, I hope you become a woman who goes where she is valued, who trusts in God's plans for her, who listens to her own heart, and who carries the strength to walk away gracefully, wishing others well, forever grateful for the lessons. Become the woman who brings depth to the world, who gives peace in her presence, who honors the man God has chosen for her, who has boundaries, and who pours love into herself until God sends the one worthy of receiving it. Protect your peace and know that not everyone deserves your softness. You do not need to beg to be understood, because God knows what lays within your heart. Pain is not punishment; it is purification. And I hope you know that being a woman who thrives in solitude, in companionship with Him, is far more powerful than seeking validation from the world. Being alone does not mean being unloved. It means being free.

## The Art of Being Preserved– Eleni Sophia

Cultivating a life of peace requires much time in solitude, but never loneliness, always in His company, shielded by His forgiveness and love. It's a life where you've taken time to know yourself, where every solo coffee isn't just a solo date, it's where every sip nourishes your body, every thought is creating your future, and every intentional moment in His company becomes co-creation.

Not everyone who has access to you should have access to your inner world. A Godly woman protects what is sacred, and she knows her home is the most sacred thing she will ever possess, not just the four walls that shelter her, but the home within herself.

Self-approval and inner order are her biggest priorities. She is an integral vessel of her home, one who brings life into the world and speaks life into those she loves. She was sent by her Creator as a vessel, chosen to use her softness to heal, to nurture, and to remind others of God's presence through her gentleness. Her grace is not weakness; it is divine strength expressed quietly, restoring everything she touches back to love. She's an integral part of her home and that's why she protects what she loves so fiercely.

## The Art of Being Preserved– Eleni Sophia

For the woman who's praying for alignment but still holding onto what she knows isn't clean. Let go. Purify. Become her. You cannot ask God to ordain something holy whilst not keeping your soul clean and your intentions pure. You want divine protection, but you still go where He never sent you. You want divine protection, but you'd rather sit at a table that doesn't reflect your values than sit with God. At some point, you must become comfortable in His presence. You must become the woman who minds her business, focuses on becoming a better her so God can give you what was always meant for your highest, most heaven-aligned self.

The Art of Being Preserved– Eleni Sophia

Sometimes you have to be honest with yourself and say, 'I'm not loved here. I'm not respected here. I'm not safe here' then walk away and never look back. When you do this, I promise you, God protects you. Because in stepping away from your comfort zone, you show your trust in Him and there's nothing He loves more than someone who puts their faith in Him, especially when stepping into the unknown.

## The Art of Being Preserved— Eleni Sophia

Being God's girl looks like saying 'no' to what disconnects you from Him, even if it means being alone. Praying before you panic, speaking to Him before you overshare and being wise enough not to overshare. Dressing like you know the angels are watching too. You are someone's wife, not the world's wife. Knowing God wants you to enjoy your life. There's nothing weak about being the woman God created to nurture, love and build legacy. She's private. She's present. She's protected. She's God's girl.

### The Art of Being Preserved— Eleni Sophia

A Godly woman knows she cannot find true peace with any hatred in her heart. She does not want anyone else's life, she doesn't wish harm on anyone, she only desires what God has called her to. And so, her biggest priority became peace, the kind that came from Him alone, untouched by the world. So, she removed herself. Isolated herself in His company alone and together, they thrived. Her contentment confuses the world but when God transforms you completely, being misunderstood becomes a quiet part of the process. Her only priority is becoming the woman God called her to be, with the purest intentions of them all. And in choosing Him first, she's finding peace the world could never give.

### The Art of Being Preserved— Eleni Sophia

If something didn't work out for you, I hope you know how much potential God sees within you, how much growth He still wants to bring forth through you. He's giving you this sacred opportunity to become a wiser, stronger, softer version of yourself. He's going to rebuild you right in front of those who underestimated you, right in front of those who did everything they could to break you down. That's the power women like you hold; you're so divinely protected that even when others plot your downfall, heaven turns it into your elevation. Every attempt against you becomes a stage for your becoming. And as you flow through life with this mindset, I hope you know how protected you are.

## The Art of Being Preserved– Eleni Sophia

Sometimes God will give you exactly what you asked for just so you can realize you deserve more. What once felt like a blessing can become a lesson, and the woman you're becoming is learning to recognize the difference. It's not ungrateful to outgrow what you once wanted. It's alignment. The version of you who prayed for that relationship, that friendship, that opportunity, she didn't know what you know now. She didn't carry the wisdom you carry today. She didn't yet understand the depth of her own worth. You are allowed to evolve beyond what you once thought you needed. You are allowed to rise.

## The Art of Being Preserved— Eleni Sophia

When your life is ordained by God, it will confuse those who move without His instruction. Don't be saddened by their misunderstanding. When your identity is anchored in who God says you are, not in who left, not in who doubted you, not in the timeline you imagined, but in the path He chose for you, you stop chasing clarity from people who can't hear what God whispered over your life. This woman walks differently. Steady, softened, sure. When your worth is rooted in heaven, nothing earthly can shake you. This world is temporary. She doesn't need to prove herself. She is already chosen. Already loved. Already becoming. Even in silence, she trusts that God is still speaking, still guiding, still working all things for her good. There's no confusion in her soul because her identity is built on Him. Her space is guarded. Her peace is protected. Her heart is continuously purified. The woman who chooses to cleanse her heart instead of gossiping, who prays over her future instead of plotting revenge, who forgives quietly and heals sacredly, she is forever protected.
A woman who walks with Him will always win.

## The Art of Being Preserved— Eleni Sophia

A woman who walks her path closely with God, hand in hand with her Creator, will always win. He's got her covered in ways no one else ever could. He adores her so much that no matter what obstacles come her way, no matter how chaotic or uncertain her life might look from the outside, she's never without direction. He's guiding her every step, even when it feels unclear. She doesn't need the world's understanding or approval; she just needs Him. And the beautiful thing is, He's always enough. Her safety, her clarity, her strength, it all comes from that divine closeness. She walks with Him; she will always win.

### The Art of Being Preserved– Eleni Sophia

When your heart is sincere, God will always honour it. He will move mountains you didn't even know were in your way. He will soften paths that once felt impossible. He will align opportunities you never imagined. A woman with a pure heart is never overlooked. God sees every unseen effort, every private tear, every quiet prayer whispered before bed. She doesn't need to force anything. She doesn't beg, chase, or plead. What is meant for her arrives gently. Because God recognizes the hearts that recognize Him.

## The Art of Being Preserved— Eleni Sophia

The world can be a very miserable place, and that's why protecting your inner world is so important. In a culture that shares the secrets that should remain within the four walls of your home, I hope you never forget how much sacredness lies in the power of your privacy. What is hidden and protected often holds the greatest value. In a world where many openly tear down their husband's name, I hope you know how much strength you hold when you choose loyalty and prayer instead. There is divine power in being a woman who protects what she loves. In a world consumed by the illusion that everyone around you wants the best for you, I hope you never forget the strength in rising above the noise and running to the One who created you.

### The Art of Being Preserved– Eleni Sophia

A woman who keeps her heart clean cannot be touched by the bitterness of the world. A woman who protects her spirit cannot be broken by the chaos around her. And a woman who walks with God can never be moved by anything that was never meant for her. Because everything that tries to disrupt her peace will only redirect her back to Him.

### The Art of Being Preserved– Eleni Sophia

There's something special about a woman who doesn't dwell when things don't go her way. Who allows herself to feel, to be sad for a moment but then she prays. She finds her peace in knowing that if something didn't come to her, it wasn't meant to protect her; it wasn't for her highest good. Even if she wanted it deeply, with all her heart, she trusts His plan enough to know that what she thought was good might've held something that could've destroyed her. For He sees what she cannot, and she finds peace in knowing He's taking care of her, always. And when God knows how pure your intentions are, He always moves with your best interest at heart. She knows this. She trusts this. She lives by this. And that's why she no longer begs for what isn't hers. She doesn't chase what walked away. She doesn't try to make sense of silence. Her soul is too aligned to force what isn't ordained. Her peace is guarded; God is her bestie.

# The Art of Being Preserved

This period is not a denial, it's a preservation. God is not keeping anything from you; He is keeping you for something He has already written in your name. When a woman carries this much purpose, He cannot release her into just anything. He protects her in ways she may not understand at first, but one day she will look back and realize that every delay was divine protection. Every closed door was a shield. Every moment she felt overlooked was God placing her somewhere higher, quieter, and safer. This season is not an absence of blessings; it is the preparation for blessings that require a woman of depth, purity, and spiritual maturity. You are being refined so that when the life He has written for you arrives, it does not overwhelm you, it fits you.

God preserves women like you because He knows your heart. He knows its softness, its sincerity, its devotion. And when your heart is this pure, He treats it like something precious. There are things He will not allow near you, people He will not permit to access you, and paths He will not let you walk, not because you are unworthy but because you are *chosen*. He is shaping you in silence, strengthening you in ways you don't even see, and preparing you for a life that requires the version of you that is emerging right now.

### The Art of Being Preserved– Eleni Sophia

This period where nothing seems to be happening is where everything is happening. You are not stagnant; you are being sanctified. God is clearing your spirit, sharpening your intuition, protecting your softness, and reminding you that what is meant for you does not need to be rushed, chased, or forced. It will arrive in its perfect time, and when it does, you will see exactly why He preserved you. You will see why He didn't let you settle, why He pulled you away from environments that dimmed your light, why He removed people who could not carry the weight of your destiny, why He closed chapters you tried so hard to keep open.

This is not denial. This is not rejection. This is God saying, 'You are too sacred to be placed anywhere prematurely.' And the woman who walks with *this* level of trust in His timing will always come out on top. She becomes a living demonstration of the power of walking through life with unwavering faith. She becomes the woman He was preserving all along.

## The Art of Being Preserved– Eleni Sophia

When you choose the man God has for you, his leadership will feel like safety. You'll trust the way he leads your home, and you'll rest in his decisions with ease. To align with this, you must take care of yourself. When God sees you honouring the vessel He created, He begins preparing the one He chose for you too. You align with the man God has for you by listening to your intuition. When you move through your days doing what brings you joy, when your heart stays pure and your intentions remain sincere, when your conversations with God become your foundation, you start attracting what is meant for you. Every day becomes a chance to refine the masterpiece you are. And when your life shifts from asking, 'What will they think?' to asking, 'What would God say?', you step into alignment with the love He wrote for you.

## The Art of Being Preserved– Eleni Sophia

A woman of God's energy is sacred. There's an exclusivity she carries that can't be replicated. God saves women like this for men who are truly worthy. Even in solitude, she trusts His timing, knowing that while God prepares her heart, He's preparing his too.

### The Art of Being Preserved– Eleni Sophia

To the good woman at heart, you know your power. You love deeply, give intentionally, and carry yourself with quiet strength. Please don't be sad just because you haven't found your person yet. Good women don't get cuffed quickly; they get chosen intentionally. Just because it happened for others before you, it doesn't mean it won't happen for you. God has an incredible plan for your life, and I don't want you to forget that. This waiting is not a reflection of your worth. God sees you for the woman you are. He's preparing you for something greater. He knows you're too sacred to be placed in the wrong hands, so He's making you wait a little longer. Not because you're behind, but because what's coming for you is too precious to be rushed.

You do everything with intention, your love, your words, your presence. I hope you're using this time alone to nurture your mind, strengthen your body, and become the best version of yourself. Because when it does happen, and it will, it won't just be love.
It will be a life worth staying for.

### The Art of Being Preserved— Eleni Sophia

And as you keep choosing a God-ordained life, I hope you know He's working to give you His best. You've never abandoned yourself in moments that could have rewritten your character. You kept choosing what felt true, not what felt convenient. You kept listening for His guidance, even when it meant walking alone. There's a specific reward for women who move through seasons of uncertainty with this kind of quiet loyalty to themselves. Let yourself rest in the certainty that He's aligning everything in your favour.

The Creator never overlooks a woman who preserves what is sacred within her.

### The Art of Being Preserved— Eleni Sophia

I know you miss her, the girl you used to be, and I understand. It's okay to mourn her. It's okay to feel that loss. But I pray the walls you've built around your heart are torn down one day, not by force, but by a love so pure and unexpected it changes everything. I pray this love, whether it comes from someone else or from within yourself, gives you the safety and freedom to soften again. You're healing. You're growing. You're becoming someone even more extraordinary than you ever imagined. You're exactly where you're meant to be.

## The Art of Being Preserved– Eleni Sophia

Your union will be made in the eyes and hands of God. It won't be rushed, forced, or born from confusion. It will come together with grace, in divine timing, when both hearts are ready to honour what is sacred. Every prayer and every moment of surrender is preparing you for this. And when it arrives, you'll know. It will feel like peace, purpose, and protection all at once. And you will finally know what it feels like to *exhale*.

### The Art of Being Preserved– Eleni Sophia

I hope nobody makes you feel a way for not participating in the small pleasures of the outside world. When people ask, 'Why don't you date?', I hope you remember that you don't belong to everybody. Women like you were created in the image of God's eyes, and He's saving you for someone just as wonderful as you. Do you really think this season is going to waste? Do you think all the times you've longed to give your love, or felt behind while everyone else dated and settled, were for nothing? You waited for the man God wrote for you.

Do you know how much exclusivity that carries?

### The Art of Being Preserved— Eleni Sophia

The most sacred transformations happen in the quiet. When your prayers feel unanswered, when your path feels misunderstood, when your presence feels out of place, know that you're being set apart, not left behind. You were never meant to fit in. The woman who walks closely with God, who finds comfort in solitude, who chooses purity in a loud world, do you know how deeply He honors that? There is a softness in your soul that the world may not notice, but heaven sees it clearly. God heard you when no one else did. He understood what you couldn't explain. Solitude with Him isn't loneliness. It's preparation. It's protection. And it's the safest place your soul can rest, rise, and become. The most sacred transformations happen in the quiet.

## The Art of Being Preserved– Eleni Sophia

Isolation is God's refinement. It's where He has space to do His best work. Not because He was ever incapable, but because for the first time, you've given Him room. You've stopped micromanaging the outcome and you've made space for Him to move in ways you can't yet see. He can finally pour into you fully. He can begin rearranging even better than all that you desire. Not because He changed, but because you did. When you walk in faith, you stop trying to control every step. You stop forcing, chasing, proving. You begin to trust the process as much as the promise. And in that quiet, in that surrender, He begins to do what only He can do. Isolation isn't absence; yes, it may feel lonely at times, but it's a step towards alignment. It's where He prepares you in private for a life that can only be carried by a woman who knows she is held.

## The Art of Being Preserved– Eleni Sophia

The best gift you could ever give your husband is you - raw and authentic you - and this is not an outdated belief. Make your soul the purest and most beautiful thing about you. A woman who walks with God cares more about being respected than anything else. A Godly woman is pure in intention, steady in heart, and full of gratitude. She knows that her femininity, her level-headedness, and her grace all come from the innocence within. The best women seek validation from their Lord and Him alone.

### The Art of Being Preserved– Eleni Sophia

And when he arrives, you'll finally understand what it feels like to be with someone who is unwaveringly certain about you. You'll remember what it feels like to smile again, held by someone who treasures you wholeheartedly. You'll relearn the feeling of joy. This is the beginning of one of the greatest transformations of your life. Keep investing in yourself. Everything will fall into place.

## The Art of Being Preserved– Eleni Sophia

A truly Godly woman who is in tune with her highest self knows her greatest asset is her femininity, her ability to bring sanctity to her space and guard her home from anything that doesn't support her husband, her children, or her happiness. She shields her home in prayer. She works on her projects. She fills her kitchen with foods that nourish her family so they can thrive. She lends her husband an arm when all he ever needed was a hand. She speaks kindness into him and builds with him. This is the girl who turns a house into a home, who brings peace into chaos, who carries warmth wherever she goes. She invests in her mind, her growth, and her faith. She's the girl whose presence feels like sunlight, whose kindness lingers, whose softness soothes. That's the girl you marry. The one who embodies grace, warmth, and strength. The one whose heart is as beautiful as her soul. She's not just any girl; she's the girl who becomes a wife. The one who turns your life into something whole, your home into something sacred, and your blessings into abundance. She is the best asset you will ever have.

### The Art of Being Preserved– Eleni Sophia

When you meet a woman who is naturally soft, softly spoken, softly strong, you'll notice how her angelic energy is rooted in her purity. Know that she's the one given to you by God. She's the one who will always want the best for you, who will give you an arm when you need a hand and the peace you've always prayed for. Treat her with gentle care, because she is a reflection of God's grace and a living embodiment of divine favour. Her prayers have protected you more times than you can imagine.

You will be someone's best thing one day, his unanswered prayer. But for now, become your own.

## The Art of Being Preserved– Eleni Sophia

God is preparing you for a sacred man, and I hope you're using this season to become the woman who will stand beside him. A union created and protected by God requires a woman who uses her time wisely, who understands that delay is not denial, and that her presence alone can transform the man God has chosen for her. God is probably looking at you both right now thinking, not yet, because He's refining you for each other. When you walk with this level of intention, everything falls into divine order. God wants you to sit with yourself until your intuition becomes sharp enough to sense what is best for the one He's chosen for you, to recognise people with impure intentions before they ever try to approach your home. A wise woman knows not everyone deserves access to what is sacred. As you wait with intention, remember this delay is one of the most divine moments of your life. It's your time to prepare for the duties God has written for you. While he works hard to provide, God wants you to work on your own goals, to build the body you've dreamed of, to nurture your gifts so He can align the two of you in His timing.

### The Art of Being Preserved– Eleni Sophia

Patience. God is preparing him too <3
To the woman who yearns to be a wife, I want you to know that everything is aligning for you. Keep working on yourself; each day is an opportunity to grow, evolve, and become the best version of who you are meant to be. Your journey isn't about waiting; it is about preparing. God's plan has always been greater than yours, remember? You may feel ready, completely prepared to love, to build, to enter the next chapter of your life, but God may still be working on him. Because when the two of you meet, you won't just be partners, you will be a team. A union built on strength, intention, and divine timing. God is shaping him into a man who will cherish you, lead with wisdom, and walk beside you with purpose. He is becoming the man who will feel like home to your heart. This is your sign that everything is working in your favour. Keep becoming. Keep trusting. Keep your heart open. Do the work, have faith, and let God do what only He can. Patience. God is preparing him too <3

## The Art of Being Preserved– Eleni Sophia

And as you walk in your anointing, talk to God. Tell Him you're excited to meet the man He has chosen for you. Praying for your husband is one of the purest expressions of love. There is something sacred about praying for a man you haven't yet met, a man whose spirit your heart recognizes through faith alone. Many want to be wives, but few understand the calling it takes to become one. Protecting a man's peace, covering his home in prayer, and carrying him in faith even before you know his name is a divine strength. When you pray for him, you are not just preparing for your future; you are showing God that you trust His timing. You thank Him for shaping both of you, for refining you into the woman who will stand beside the man He has chosen for you. And when it is time, your love will feel like coming home. Not a meeting, but a remembering.

## The Art of Being Preserved— Eleni Sophia

In your faith, he will find peace. In your softness, he will find courage. You will become the reason he keeps going. You will create a sense of calm within your home, knowing that what is sacred between you stays between you, him, and the One who created you both. No competition. No pressure. Pure trust. And from your union will come a family that is shielded, a home that is anointed, and a love that stands as quiet proof of His perfect timing.

## The Art of Being Preserved– Eleni Sophia

That's the girl you marry. One day you will meet a girl who is closest to God, the one who keeps her relationship with Him so sacred that it becomes her greatest protection. She's the girl who runs to God when things feel heavy, placing her trust in His guidance. On the days you argue, He will be the first place she turns, praying for clarity and asking Him to guide you both back to one another. You will never see her sharing your vulnerabilities with others or speaking ill of you. She will honour you, even in your absence, valuing you for the man you are. She won't give up on you. She will support your dreams in ways no one ever has. Her energy will captivate you. She'll become your quiet motivation, the force that strengthens you without saying a word. Around this girl, life becomes magical. She will bring peace to your chaos, joy to your struggles, and light to your darkest days. She will stand beside you with unwavering loyalty, believing in you with a depth no one else has ever shown you. This is the girl whose prayers have been covering you long before you met. Her heart is pure, her intentions sincere, and her spirit is her most beautiful asset. She may not be the loudest person in the room, but her kindness is unforgettable, and her soul carries a quiet peace that feels like home.

The Art of Being Preserved— Eleni Sophia

Every prayer you whisper for your future husband shields him from things he may never know. Every time you choose patience over worry, purity over distraction, or faith over fear, you are covering him in protection. God hears every word. He sees every tear. He watches your surrender, and He is using it all to strengthen the man who will one day lead, love, and protect you and your home. Your prayers are building the foundation of a union shaped and sustained by His hands.

The Art of Being Preserved– Eleni Sophia

Do you know how much purity lies in the ability to pray for a man you haven't met yet? To love him through faith alone, to cover him in prayer without knowing his name, his face, or the sound of his voice? That kind of love is sacred. It is patient, selfless, and deeply rooted in trust. It reveals a heart led by God, a woman who believes in divine timing and knows what's meant for her will arrive when her soul is ready. There is holiness in your waiting, grace in your longing, and power in every prayer whispered for the man who will one day call you his.

The Art of Being Preserved— Eleni Sophia

The power of a woman of faith is unmatched. She is the calm in your chaos, the anchor in your storms, the guardian of your secrets, and the protector of your home's peace. She sees your ambition and prays for your success. Within her, solitude becomes sanctuary and tranquillity becomes a luxury. Together, you build your kingdom, knowing the woman beside you is an alchemist, someone who turns the ordinary into something blessed.

## The Art of Being Preserved– Eleni Sophia

I hope you find the courage to build a life you are truly obsessed with, one that feels aligned with your spirit and rich with purpose. A life where you surprise yourself with your resilience, your growth, and your capacity to rise. When you believe you're destined for more, more will always find you. I can't wait for you to leave every doubter in awe. The ones who projected their fears onto you, the ones who tried to interfere, the ones who didn't understand you. That is the power of a woman who truly trusts herself. She always wins.

Forever the girl who is reached by few, misunderstood by many but always connected to her own soul.

## The Art of Being Preserved– Eleni Sophia

The Art of Being Preserved– Eleni Sophia

## Also, by Eleni Sophia

**'This One's for You'** a poetry collection about the power of self-love and finding oneself.

**'Perspective by Sophia'-** a motivational book, where Sophia simplifies the 'law of attraction' and encourages you on living a life that you love, just by changing your mindsets!

**'Good Morning to Goodnight'** the rawest collection about 'love' and first heartbreak.

**'Breaking the Cycle'** a collection of the power of breaking generational cycles, embracing your femininity and the beauty in balancing a career and motherhood.

## The Art of Being Preserved– Eleni Sophia

She's the type of woman you know is going to have it all. Just one look at her and you know. Not because other people believe in her, but because she believes in herself. She's the one breaking all the generational curses; she's known as the 'rule breaker and the troublemaker.' And she's okay with that. The outside noise is just noise. We often hear, 'Tradition is nothing but advice from the dead' and my goodness, how true is that?! She's forever the protector of her future home, partner, and children. And as she becomes aligned and in tune with her higher self, she embodies her truth. Clothed in self-love, filled with ambition, and protected. You'll fall in love with her magic. She knows she will have it all.

**– Breaking the Cycle by Eleni Sophia**

Wish them the very best And let them walk away If they don't want to be a part of your life anymore Maybe, it's time for this particular journey to end. And I know it's hard It is so incredibly hard. You're left wondering what you did wrong But I urge you to shift your perspective. If you can give so much compassion to the wrong one Think about how much you will be able to give to the one meant for you. The fact that you were able to show so much emotion shows how much you can love, and that is truly magnificent.
Maybe one day you will cross paths grown and evolved You will look back with clarity and realize why things happened

If they are meant to be in your life Inevitably, It will happen.
For now, Continue to put yourself first It's finally time to start making yourself a priority Putting your happiness first. You deserve everything this world has to offer and more Learn to give it to yourself first You will see why.
**– This One's for You by Eleni Sophia**

## About the Publisher:

Perspective Press Global is an independent publishing firm representing authors under the age of 20.

At Perspective Press Global, our mission is to inspire young aspiring authors that there is no such thing as being 'too young;' your voices deserve to be heard.

The firm was founded based on Sophia's struggle to find representation when she was a 13-year-old writer. We now have published young talent from around the globe – including, the UK, Albania, Kosovo, Ireland, and Australia!

If you're interested in joining our team, please visit our submissions page at perspectivepressglobal.com and come say hello over on Instagram @PerspectivePressGlobal

Signed copies of all books can be found on perspectivepressglobal.com

For Eleni Sophia's work follow @EleniiSophia

Copyright © 2025 Eleni Sophia

The Art of Being Preserved

All rights reserved.

ISBN: 978-1-914275-59-3

Perspective Press Global Ltd

www.ingramcontent.com/pod-product-compliance
Lightning Source LLC
Chambersburg PA
CBHW060457080526
44584CB00015B/1461